GIGANOTOSAURUS

AND OTHER BIG DINOSAURS

by Dougal Dixon

illustrated by
Steve Weston and James Field

PICTURE WINDOW BOOKS
Minneapolis, Minnesota

Picture Window Books
5115 Excelsior Boulevard
Suite 232
Minneapolis, MN 55416
877-845-8392
www.picturewindowbooks.com

Printed in the United States of America.

Library of Congress Cataloging-in-Publication Data
Dixon, Dougal.
Giganotosaurus and other big dinosaurs / by
Dougal Dixon ; illustrated by Steve Weston & James
Field.
p. cm. – (Dinosaur find)
Includes bibliographical references and index.
ISBN 1-4048-1325-X
1. Dinosaurs—Size—Juvenile literature.
2. Giganotosaurus—Size—Juvenile literature.
I. Weston, Steve, ill. II. Field, James, 1959- ill. III. Title.
QE861.5.D5927 2006
567.9—dc22   2005023329

Acknowledgments
This book was produced for Picture Window Books by
Bender Richardson White, U.K.

Illustrations by James Field (pages cover and 4–5, 7,
11, 15, 19) and Steve Weston (pages 9, 13, 17, 21).
Diagrams by Stefan Chabluk.
All photographs copyright Digital Vision.

Consultant: John Stidworthy, Scientific Fellow of
the Zoological Society, London, and former
Lecturer in the Education Department, Natural
History Museum, London.

Reading Adviser: Susan Kesselring, M.A., Literacy
Educator, Rosemount-Apple Valley-Eagan
(Minnesota) School District

Types of dinosaurs
In this book, a red shape at the
top of a left-hand page shows
the animal was a meat-eater.
A green shape shows it was
a plant-eater.

Just how big—or small—
were they?
Dinosaurs were many different
sizes. We have compared their
sizes to one of the following:

Chicken
2 feet (60 centimeters) tall
6 pounds (2.7 kilograms)

Adult person
6 feet (1.8 meters) tall
170 pounds (76.5 kg)

Elephant
10 feet (3 m) tall
12,000 pounds
(5,400 kg)

TABLE OF CONTENTS

The Biggest Dinosaurs . . .4
Sauroposeidon 6
Giganotosaurus 8
Spinosaurus 10
Sauropelta 12
Seismosaurus 14
Argentinosaurus 16

Shantungosaurus 18
Torosaurus 20
Where Did They Go? . .22
Glossary 23
To Learn More 24
Index 24

WHAT'S INSIDE?

Dinosaurs lived between 230 and
65 million years ago. These dinosaurs
were some of the biggest. Find out how
they lived and what they have in
common with today's animals.

THE BIGGEST DINOSAURS

During the middle of the Age of Dinosaurs, some of the biggest animals that ever lived walked the Earth. The largest were plant-eating dinosaurs with long necks. There must have been plenty of plants for them to eat.

Tall *Sauroposeidon* walked slowly across the plain looking for trees. They fed on leaves from the treetops. Long, low *Seismosaurus* fed on plants on the ground. These dinosaurs were always on the lookout for giant meat-eaters that would attack them.

SAUROPOSEIDON

Sauroposeidon was so big that it could not push its way between the trees of the forests. It had to stay along the edges where there was room to move around. *Sauroposeidon* lived in big herds.

Big herds today

Elephants move in herds like *Sauroposeidon* did. They travel through forests and across open plains.

Size Comparison

The tall necks of *Sauroposeidon* helped them to see any meat-eaters that were coming to attack them.

GIGANOTOSAURUS

Pronunciation:
JY-ga-NO-toe-SAW-rus

Giganotosaurus was the biggest meat-eating dinosaur that has been discovered. It was even bigger than the famous *Tyrannosaurus*. It hunted and ate the enormous long-necked plant-eating dinosaurs that lived at that time.

Big hunter today

The tiger is so large and strong that, like *Giganotosaurus*, most other animals are frightened by it.

Size Comparison

Giganotosaurus had huge teeth and enormous jaws. The *Giganotosaurus* could bite into and tear apart the biggest plant-eaters.

9

SPINOSAURUS

Pronunciation:
SPINE-o-SAW-rus

The massive sail on the back of *Spinosaurus* made the dinosaur look much bigger than it was. *Spinosaurus* could use its sail for signaling to its friends and its enemies.

River hunter today

A crocodile is a fierce hunter. Its long jaws and teeth allow it to eat meat and fish like *Spinosaurus* once did.

Size Comparison

Spinosaurus lived on the banks of rivers. It would dip its long jaws into the water to catch fish with its many teeth.

11

Sauropelta was a huge plant-eater. Its back was covered in armor to protect it from big meat-eaters. *Sauropelta* was too heavy to fight or to run away, but the armor kept it safe against teeth and claws of mighty meat-eaters.

Armor today

A giant tortoise is safe inside its shell, just like *Sauropelta* was safe under its armor.

Size Comparison

Sauropelta was one of the biggest of the armored dinosaurs. Meat-eaters would think twice about attacking this spiky beast.

SEISMOSAURUS

Pronunciation:
SIZE-mo-SAW-rus

Seismosaurus was perhaps the longest dinosaur that ever lived. It was the length of three school buses. It had a long neck, a small head, and a whiplike tail. Its body was slim and its legs were short.

Long necks today

Giraffes have long necks and small heads like *Seismosaurus* did. They also move in herds and feed on the leaves of trees and bushes.

Size Comparison

14

Seismosaurus means "earthquake lizard." When a herd of *Seismosaurus* was on the move, the ground shook.

15

ARGENTINOSAURUS

Pronunciation:
ARE-jen-TEEN-o-SAW-rus

Argentinosaurus was probably the heaviest dinosaur that ever lived. It was three times heavier than *Seismosaurus*. Its legs were like treetrunks, which was necessary to support such a heavy body.

African elephants

Elephants are big, heavy plant-eaters and tower over other animals like *Argentinosaurus* did.

Size Comparison

Argentinosaurus was a plant-eater. With its long neck, it could reach up to eat in the tops of the tallest trees that grew at that time.

SHANTUNGOSAURUS

Pronunciation:
SHAN-tung-uh-SAW-rus

Shantungosaurus had a beak like the beak of a duck. But the dinosaur was far, far bigger than any duck. Its head was almost as big as you, its body was enormous, and it had a long, thick tail.

Big heads today

Bison have big heads and wide mouths. They eat low-growing plants like *Shantungosaurus* did.

Size Comparison

Shantungosaurus probably ate buds and small plants that grew close to the ground. It would have used its broad beak to rip them up like a giant lawn mower.

TOROSAURUS

Pronunciation:
TOR-uh-SAW-rus

Among the last dinosaurs were the kinds that had heads covered in armor and horns. *Torosaurus* had the biggest head of all the dinosaurs we know. With an armored shield at the back, its head was 9 feet (2.7 m) long.

Horns today

A rhinoceros uses its big head and its horns to scare off enemies like *Torosaurus* did millions of years ago.

Size Comparison

Torosaurus had three horns on its head. It also had a shield that stretched back over its shoulders. The shield protected its neck against attack by meat-eating dinosaurs.

WHERE DID THEY GO?

Dinosaurs are extinct, which means that none of them are alive today. Scientists study rocks and fossils to find clues about what happened to dinosaurs.

People have different explanations about what happened. Some people think a huge asteroid hit Earth and caused all sorts of climate changes, which caused the dinosaurs to die. Others think volcanic eruptions caused the climate to change and that killed the dinosaurs. No one knows for sure what happened to all the dinosaurs.

GLOSSARY

armor—protective covering of plates, horns, spikes, or clubs used for fighting

beak—the hard front part of the mouth of birds and some dinosaurs

claws—tough, usually curved fingernails or toenails

herds—large groups of animals that move, feed, and sleep together

horns—pointed structures on the head

plains—large areas of flat land with few large plants

sail—tall, thin, upright structure on the back of some animals

signaling—making a sign, warning, or hint

To Learn More

At the Library

Clark, Neil, and William Lindsay. *1001 Facts About Dinosaurs.* New York: Backpack Books, Dorling Kindersley, 2002.

Dixon, Dougal. *Dougal Dixon's Amazing Dinosaurs.* Honesdale, Penn.: Boyds Mills Press, 2000.

Holtz, Thomas, and Michael Brett-Surman. *Jurassic Park Institute Dinosaur Field Guide.* New York: Random House, 2001.

On the Web

FactHound offers a safe, fun way to find Web sites related to this book. All of the sites on FactHound have been researched by our staff.

1. Visit *www.facthound.com*
2. Type in this special code: 140481325X
3. Click on the FETCH IT button.

Your trusty FactHound will fetch the best sites for you!

Look for all of the books in the Dinosaur Find series:

Ankylosaurus and Other Mountain Dinosaurs 1-4048-0670-9
Centrosaurus and Other Dinosaurs of Cold Places 1-4048-0672-5
Ceratosaurus and Other Fierce Dinosaurs 1-4048-1327-6
Deltadromeus and Other Shoreline Dinosaurs 1-4048-0669-5
Giganotosaurus and Other Big Dinosaurs 1-4048-1325-X
Ornithomimus and Other Fast Dinosaurs 1-4048-1326-8

Plateosaurus and Other Desert Dinosaurs 1-4048-0667-9
Saltopus and Other First Dinosaurs 1-4048-1328-4
Scutellosaurus and Other Small Dinosaurs 1-4048-1330-6
Stegosaurus and Other Plains Dinosaurs 1-4048-0668-7
Styracosaurus and Other Last Dinosaurs 1-4048-1329-2
Triceratops and Other Forest Dinosaurs 1-4048-0671-7

Index

Argentinosaurus, 16–17
armor, 12, 13, 20
beak, 18, 19
claws, 12
Giganotosaurus, 8–9
herds, 6, 14, 15
jaws, 9, 10, 11

meat-eaters, 5, 8, 12, 13, 21
neck, 4, 7, 8, 14, 17, 21
plant-eaters, 4, 8, 9, 12, 16, 17
Sauropelta, 12–13
Sauroposeidon, 5, 6–7

Seismosaurus, 5, 14–15, 16
Shantungosaurus, 18–19
Spinosaurus, 10–11
tail, 14, 18
Torosaurus, 20–21
Tyrannosaurus, 8